Fly Like an Eagle

Sharing Christian Insights and Interpreting Visions

By Jessie Schlaser

Fly Like an Eagle

ISBN-13: 978-1530558872
ISBN-10: 1530558875

First Edition, March 2016

Published by
Groundwaters Publishing, LLC

P.O. Box 50, Lorane, Oregon 97451
http://www.groundwaterspublishing.com

Dedication

I dedicate this book to my husband Fred who has always been by my side with faith and love. He encouraged me to continue my education and follow my dream of ministering to others.

To God the Father who has always been my rock and guide with unconditional love.

To Pat Edwards who was a great help in putting my words into this beautiful book.

Thank you, Jessie

Fly Like An Eagle

> *But those who wait on the Lord shall renew their strength; they shall mount up with wings like Eagles; they shall run and not be weary; they shall walk and not be faint.   Isaiah 40:31 NKJV*

Eagles ~ observant, watchful, on guard, listening, discerning

• Eagles have keen vision. They can see prey up to two miles away
• Eagles are fearless. They seldom surrender to size or strength
• Eagles are tenacious. They never give up -- taking advantage of every storm by flying with the wind
• Eagles are high flyers and wait for opportunities to strike
• Eagles are not scavengers
• Eagles are monogamous. They mate for life.
• Eagles nurture their young. Although aggressors, they are gentle and attentive to their young. They teach the young to fly and grow to their potential.

Table of Contents

Dedication
Foreword
Introduction
Prelude

Chapter One

Chapter Two

Chapter Three

Chapter Four

Chapter Five

Foreword

It is with great pleasure that I can write to you so you can share this at Jessie's celebration for her wonderful accomplishments of earning her Associate's Degree and her Certificate of Ministry.

I first became acquainted with Jessie when she was assigned to me as a Christian Leadership University student several years ago. I admire anyone her age who continues with their education and has special goals they still want to accomplish instead of thinking they are too old to learn "new tricks!"

So I admire Jessie! Even though the studies haven't been easy for her, I was blessed by her tenacity and diligence to press through the difficulties until she reached her goal. She is to be complimented and celebrated.

Jessie is truly a Christian mystic with visionary and hearing abilities she has developed by walking with the Lord for many years. Jessie is a prophetess since she hears from God and can relay His message to others. Jessie is an intercessor who cares deeply for people. Her concerns for others have led her to host classes in which to teach them how to cast their burdens on the Lord and to be able to receive His love and guidance.

Jessie is an author. If you haven't read her book, *Wait, Listen, Record,* be sure to get a copy. It was a tremendous blessing to me, and I know it will be to you also!

Cherish Jessie for she has much to offer you.

In Christian love,
Rev. Dr. Karen Joy King, Ph.D.
Christian Leadership University Professor

IF GOD HAD VOICE MAIL

Most of us have now learned to live with "voice mail" as a necessary part of our daily lives. But, have you ever wondered what it would be like if God decided to install "voice mail?" Imagine praying and hearing the following:

- Thank you for calling Heaven. Press 1 for English
- Press 2 for Spanish
- For all other languages, press 0

  Please select one of the following options:

- Press 1 for Requests
- Press 2 for Thanksgiving
- Press 3 for Complaints
- Press 4 for all other inquiries.

  I am sorry. All of our angels and saints are busy helping other sinners right now. However, your prayer is important to us, and we will answer it in the order it was received. Please stay on the line.
  If you would like to speak to:

- God---press 1
- Jesus---press 2
- Holy Spirit---press 3

  If you would like to hear King David sing a Psalm while you are holding, press 4.

To find a loved one that has been assigned to Heaven, press 5, then enter his or her Kingdom security number, followed by the pound sign. If you receive a negative response, please hang up and try again.

For reservations at Heaven, please enter J-O-H-N, followed by the numbers 3-1-6.

For answers to nagging questions about dinosaurs, the age of the earth, life on other planets and where Noah's Ark is, please wait until you arrive.

Our computers show that you have already prayed today. Please hang up and try again tomorrow.

The office is now closed for the weekend to observe a religious holiday. Please pray again on Monday after 9:30 am.

If you are calling after hours and need emergency assistance, please contact your local pastor.

Thank you and have a heavenly day.

Posted on SermonCentral website
Submitted by Rev. James Hamar

Chapter One:

COLD AND DARKNESS

As we walk through the gate into the garden, I see a grove of trees. I have never seen trees in here before. They are very tall, mostly conifer type. As we walk into the forest, it has many broken limbs and debris lying on the ground; broken limbs are hanging within the trees ready to fall. It is dark and very cold and damp in here. I can't hear any birds singing; it is very quiet. There is only the sound of us breaking twigs as we walk over them.

Lord, why have we come to this cold, dark and lonely place?

This, My Daughter, is what my beautifully-created world has become. No one takes care anymore. There is much neglect of the things of worth. The people want their freedom to do it their way. If it feels right, they just do it with no concern for their fellow man – just self and greed.

I called their names over and over. I wept with my Father, but they still chose their own way. I will call my people home unto my Father very soon, for my whole earth shall become a land of death... Come, My Child, and see my beauty.

Oh, wow! Such beauty! Everything seems to glow. Every kind of plant and flower one can imagine; each so perfect, without spot or blemish. There is singing and music along with all the beautiful, colorful birds and butterflies. It is so awesome it takes your breath away. If I blink, I will surely miss something. It's the Garden of Eden before man's sin.

Tell my people to get on their faces and pray; pray as never before. Repent, prepare yourself clean and pure. The hours are so near to come unto my Father in Heaven.
He waits for his church, clean and pure.

Psalm 97, NKJ

WASTED AWAY

The garden gate is hanging by one hinge. The other is rusted away. This one is badly corroded. The steps are ruined too; some are completely over-grown with brush, some have eroded away. The pathway, too, has been neglected with ruts from the rains and grass over-grown in other areas. The gardens have so many open, vacant areas. The plants are few and many are sickly. Vast areas have just withered away.

But wait! You can see a few, very few, upright, strong and fresh looking.

Oh Lord, it looks as though no one has cared and they just wasted away. They were not tended to. Even the pool has dried up and debris lie in it.

Yes, My Daughter. This is as many of my churches, my Father's houses. They are empty and many are dead as my word has been shut out. The people only hear 'feel good' messages. Yes, they came and received prayer; some accepted me in their lives, but many are left to wander as they are not discipled.

Yes, they are taught right from wrong, but they are not receiving nourishment from my commandments. They only know about me; they do not get to know me. They don't know how to commune with me.

The body is weak and sickly.

Psalm 29, NKJ

THE VERY TALL TREES

We are walking in a forest. The trees are magnificent, so very tall and straight; so very tall, they seemingly reach into the heavens; straight as an arrow, they are. They sway with the gentle winds. If you listen, you can hear the angels singing as they sit on the limbs and branches. The music is so heavenly, but yet there is a sense of sadness.

When you turn your eye to the ground below there is no beauty; only an occasional bird hopping around searching, frantically searching, for a morsel of food.

My Lord, how can there be such a dramatic change from the trees to the earth?

These, My Child, are symbolic of my Father's kingdom. The desolate, dead earth is my people, who are hurting. They are desperate and searching, but most are looking in the wrong places. They need to look up, keep their eyes on the Kingdom, for my Father in Heaven is Life.

Humankind has turned away and against one another and are only concerned about "self."

My Father awaits with open arms.

Where Are You Walking? Where Does Your Path Take You?

Psalm 90, NKJ

SHINING FACES

I can see sunflowers, tall above the garden wall. All their faces point out and over the fence tops. They seem to watch and follow us as we walk.

These shining sunflower faces are my people... servants, walking, talking, caring for, serving for many needs... my help, my salvation.

These workers serve many needy souls. They bring comfort and my word to hurting souls. Yes, every direction you look here in the garden, you see shining spirits ready and waiting to give you my rest.

Psalm 84, NKJ

SEE THE GLORY

Jesus is waiting at the gate. He takes my hand and we walk through the gate. It's a beautiful archway covered with vines and fragrant white flowers. The fragrance is soft, heavenly. It fills the air wherever we walk. The flower gardens are especially beautiful today; a solid carpet of color everywhere you look.

Even the fountain seems to have a special glow around it today. The water falls softly but yet with new energy and a rush. You can look deep within the pool. Its crystal clear water seems to be bottomless, but we know it is only a few feet deep in reality. It's like a mirror; you can see yourself, but it's more like a mirage. You see your own image and Jesus' glory; the golden glow of his shining light. The water seems to dance and sparkle like a diamond in the sky.

We continue to walk on through the garden. I notice that in some areas, the flowers seem to droop and bend down as we looked ahead, but some would pop back up, straight, tall and in full beauty, as we approach.

This went on for several flower groupings, and curiosity got the best of me. I had to ask Jesus, "Why are they acting that way? It is almost as though they are alive."

He laughs.

You have many stumbling blocks before you. Turn around and look at the big pile over there. Those you have already overcome; these you see are much smaller, but you call upon me and you bore right through each one as you called my name. You jump right back quicker than the time before. You still have some stumbling blocks before you, but they are much smaller and fewer.

As you grow stronger, you bring those nearby up with you. That's why the drooping, bent-over flowers pop back up in pairs and group as we walk by them.

You don't walk alone. I am with you always when you call my name. Miracles happen. You just need to listen, wait and believe.

Psalm 130, NKJ

PROSPERITY

It is a beautiful day for a walk in the garden. The air is warm with a soft breeze. The flowers are at their best, some tall and erect. They are in their prime while others are all right, but not so perfect and beautiful. Some are weak and sickly-looking.

Butterflies hovering over the flowers seem to just float with the breeze, like angels circling over.

Birds – songbirds – are everywhere. Some are busy searching for food. They run and bounce like small children playing. Others seem to just hurry frantically to and fro, but not satisfying their needs. The water in the pool appears restless; ripples dance across the top of the water.

Lord, the walk is very peaceful and pleasant today, but there seems to be an uneasiness in the air. Why is that?

The tall erect flowers are prepared and ready to meet my Father in Heaven. They know that their lamps are full and their wicks are trimmed. The weaker ones are unsure, confused; they have no sure direction. They are still searching and uncertain and some are nonbelievers.

The butterflies are the angels that guide, protect and oversee. They watch over all of my people.

The birds' warehouses are full so they have plenty. They are blessed. The ones running and searching non-stop have no faith. They have turned away with unbelief, running away. They live in fear.

My Child, my Father looks down from Heaven with brokenness and weeping for the unsaved. He knows what lies ahead for them in their future.

Matthew 25: 1-13, NKJ

8

OH DEAR LORD

Oh Lord, there is so much unrest and turmoil throughout the world; so many people with insecurity, hopelessness and nowhere to turn. Major natural disasters are magnifying and multiplying throughout the world. There are droughts and floods – going from one extreme to another.

Thousands are dying daily. There are so many lost souls. Many are turning away; many have closed hearts, no remorse, and major illnesses are running rampant. They have no morals, no self-respect. Anything goes; if it feels good, they go with it.

Oh Lord, you have warned us many times in your word that these things would again come to pass. As these days grow worse, they too must come to pass.

Look up as the time grows nigh, for the great and glorious return and renewing of this world.

Oh Lord, how much longer must these times linger?

Oh My Child, these days will soon close as my return is much closer than you think. Be ready. Be prepared as I am standing at the door and the angels are at attention, ready to blow the trumpets to call my people home unto my Father.

Tell my churches to teach the people about the future that lies ahead for both the righteous and the unbelievers. Don't make it a pity party.

Tell them my words, true and firm. Prepare them. Time is very short.

Luke 21: 5-37, NKJ

9

A GIFT FROM HEAVEN

The garden is exceptionally beautiful today. So quiet, so serene. The flowers all seem to be looking my way and smiling as though they are saying, "We love you. We have come to comfort and support you in your time of need."

The flowers have such beauty and fragrance which are incomparable to anything else. Many songbirds of all varieties surround the pool. All are chirping and singing. Some are drinking; some are taking a bath in the upper bowl of water... so many birds, all in one place, all at the same time... such sweet music. Soft wispy clouds are slowly drifting in the deep blue sky.

The clouds resemble a sandy beach with soft rippling in the sand left by the waves of the seas.

The birds' sweet songs sound like angels singing all around us.

Jesus and I just stand and watch and listen as the birds run around us and land on our shoulders. Tears stream down our faces as we are blessed in this moment from our Father above in Heaven.

There is such sweet love... indescribable. Only God can give such love and beauty.

Psalm 8, NKJ

PRAYERS

My Dear Jesus:
   Oh my Lord, forgive me for my blindness. You have been trying to teach me, show me how to see you, really see you, and respond to things around me through my husband's illness and my own handicaps. I am so sorry for my blindness.

Lord, I ask you to help me retain the things I am reading and learning in this awesome book called *Living through Breast Cancer with Faith, Hope, and Laughter* by Laura Jensen Walker.

And Lord, I sincerely hope that if it is your will for me to publish my writings. I do hope and pray that they too will minister to others as this lady's book does.

No, I don't wish to imitate her; just let my writing do the talking to their hearts as hers does. Yes Lord, there is a time in our lives for everything. Help me Lord to receive what you have for me and help me to change and see you as you really are. Take me into the holy of holies and change me, Lord.

My Dear Child, I feel your sorrow. I am with you... I am holding you in my arms. I will carry you through these times. I hear your husband's cry for help. I will lift him before my Father, for his mercy is great. Be strong my child as I will give you strength for yourself and your children, for they are weak. The church will support you.

Dear Lord, I feel so helpless with my husband's and my own well-being, both physical and mental. I feel and see a large rolling cloud of dust trailing behind me, slowly moving closer and closer to knock me down to try to make me helpless and hopeless. I know this is not a good thing, but I also know that God is with me and will sustain me through anything that comes my way. If he brings me to it, he will bring me through it. I feel alone in the flesh, but I am not alone in spirit.

Whatever these coming days foretell, I am ready to face them, one by one. As my Lord walks me through.

Psalm 23, NKJ

LIVING WATER

As we walk into the garden it is a beautiful, warm sunny day. The sky is clear and deep blue. Song birds flying in the air are just moving from place to place, enjoying their freedom. There are very tall flowers everywhere of all colors and types – sunflowers, larkspur, delphiniums and some tall beautifully-colored grasses. Many are kinds that I have never seen before. They are all standing tall and erect as though they are watching and listening.

Soft music is playing in the background, and the flowers and grasses are all gently swaying in rhythm to the music. They encircle the fountain, seemingly listening to words being spoken by the water.

Living water!!

The uplifting words of encouragement and praise are spoken in picture form. You can see and feel the love and compassion in every one. Your heart melts. How can one explain such deep-felt love?

My Father speaks only love with deep compassion to his children that will hear and obey him. The color of the flowers is the inner beauty God has sealed within each of his children, each with its own brilliance of Glory.

STAND UP AND BE COUNTED

There is excitement in the air as we walk through the gate into the garden. The flowers are dancing. Flashes of light similar to lightning are shooting in all directions from each flower. There is a rumbling of music and drums as from afar.

Angels with batons of flashing colorful lights are overhead. At the fountain, the falling water sounds like harps playing in the distance. Its so beautiful; the glory of the Lord is everywhere.

Suddenly, there is darkness; stillness descends and everything stops. It is cold and an eeriness seems to overpower everything.

In spots, a little movement can be seen. Through the dark, people are crawling as though to move to a better place. Occasionally one will pop up and stand only to fall back down.

Lord, why did all this change from one extreme to another? How sad, how heartbreaking! Why? What happened to cause this terrible thing?

My Child, the beauty, the dancing, the music, the glory represent those who are awaiting my return and have prepared their souls. They are filled with my joy, love and peace.

The dark and desolate represent those who have fallen and turned away from me. They are the ones who have rejected my call and went their own ways. They played and partied, found their own joy and depended on man to fulfill and supply all their needs.

Psalm 29, NKJ

14

DEAR JESUS

Lord, your word says that you will never leave nor forsake us. I stand on your word. I know you are with us during every trial we are confronting at this time and always. I do have peace about it all. I know everything is going to be ok as, Lord, you are in charge.

Your word says if we ask in your name, believing so, it will be done. I declare that my husband, Fred, will be healed of this cancer, as you healed him when he had liver cancer. I declare this done in the name of Jesus.

Satan, you have no hold on Fred. You have lost the battle, so go back to the pit of Hell where you came from in the name of Jesus. I rebuke you and this cancer.

My Dear Child, I hear your prayer, I hear your cries. I will give you strength and peace to endure these times. I have your husband in my hand. I am guiding him through these times. This too will pass. Everything will come to pass and there is a blessing waiting at the end of these trials, for a new season lies ahead.

HEAR MY CALL

Jesus takes my hand and we walk through the garden gate together. We pause and look around. There are plants of all sizes, all mixed together. Some are sickly; others, strong and bright, and there are sunflowers everywhere. Some of the sunflowers are tall and straight; some are bent over as though they are tending to the sickly ones.

Birds are circling overhead and chirping loudly as though they are saying, "Hurry, hurry faster. The clock is about to strike midnight."

There is a big grandfather clock standing off in the distance. You can see the face and hear the ticking – tic-toc, tic-toc. It too seems to get louder with each passing minute. Many of the plants are healed with each tic-toc of the clock and they dance and sing.

Jesus and I stand and watch. Soon he speaks.

The tall sunflowers are ministering, encouraging and praying for the poor, the lonely, the lost and forgotten. These are the end times, the new season. These are the servants bringing miracles, healing and salvation.

I am opening the door wider than ever before. Those who hear my voice and obey are the ones who will bring the miracles to pass. All will see the manifestations of my words. I am preparing the hearts of those that want to be a part of these days.

Who can withstand the slander the ridiculing? I will do the work through all who answer my call.

Chapter Two

COME TO ME LITTLE CHILDREN

We are standing in the garden, there is a gentle wind. The air is filled with the fragrance of the violets. Everywhere we step are violets... blue, purple, red and white ones. They are so beautiful and fragrant. Pansies with glowing, smiling and happy faces are scattered among the violets. One hates to take a step for fear of walking on them, but they bounce right back up and not one is broken or bruised. Mixed among them are yellow daffodils – the big giant ones and the small dainty jonquils. They too are everywhere. They sway and nod as though they are dancing and praying. They seem to be almost smiling and laughing.

There are huge giant sunflowers scattered about in the garden, too. Their heads are bowed toward the ground as though in reverence, hovering over the smaller flowers.

I ask, "Lord, why are the huge sunflowers there? They seem so out of place among these smaller, delicate flowers?"

These smaller flowers are the children of the world – all sizes, colors and ages. Yes, children, the lost, forgotten, neglected and abused ones. See how they are dancing and rejoicing as they have heard and received me into their hearts.

The huge sunflowers are the evangelists, servants like you, ministering, teaching, praying for them, spreading the word and leading them to me.

THE BIG CITY

We are walking down the sidewalk in a big city. There must be hundreds of people walking by. It's a very big city like New York or Tokyo. Some are rushing as though they are late for an appointment; some are very slow, doing their best, but they too will arrive at their destination. The children are holding tight to their parents' hands so not to get separated, while the little ones are being carried or pushed in a device of some kind.

There are also many different types and varieties of mobilization. We soon come to a resting place with several benches for people to sit and rest. We found a place where we could clearly see the people walking by. We then quietly just sat and watched. Many different nationalities, ages and cultures passed by – rich and poor, young and the very old.

Some were almost running with great anxiety on their faces; they had a time schedule to meet. Some were walking normal speed with smiling, happy faces. You wonder what their thoughts are. Some are very sad with heartbroken looks on their faces, their heads lowered. Are they very ill or have they had a bad experience in life? What has hurt them so deeply?

Some walk with their heads held up high, elegantly dressed. They act like they have no cares or worries. They are on top of the mountain.

Here comes the one with head bent down, face drawn, and no expression. His clothes are dirty-looking and torn. He is carrying a small plastic bag, probably containing all his earthly possessions. I wonder if he has a bed, or where he slept last night. Was he warm enough?

Small children pass, some happily moving along while others are almost running to keep up with mom. She is in a hurry.

Others are skipping and jumping, as children do with an over-abundance of energy. The oncoming crowd of people seem to be everlasting, the lines never ending.

There are so many people, and no two are alike – no needs, wants, circumstances or lifestyle are the same. But yes, each and every one has a need, known and unknown, from the very wealthy to the very poorest. That need is to have the Lord and Savior Jesus Christ in their lives.

My Dear Child, did you notice that the number of happy smiling faces are fewer? Those are my people. They live their life in me and my commandments. I have provided their needs. They aren't looking for the treasures and fun parties of the world. They all have their needs and wants fulfilled and thank me.

The withdrawn, sad faces, are those who want more. They need more as their money doesn't reach their needs. They don't look to me for their provisions, nor do they serve me. Everything is their way, trying to do it alone with their own power. They don't want to lose their fun lifestyles to let me into their hearts.

They say "I can't live like that. I would have to give up too much. It's much too hard for me." So, they don't enter into a church; fear and greed have overcome them. No one comes by the sides of the bent and ragged ones when they need me most.

Some come from broken families of crime and immorality. They were never taught nor saw the good side of life. They are the lost and neglected ones, but not all is forever lost. There is still hope for them even though they can see no hope. Someone needs to take their hand, give them friendship and show them some of my love.

Help them find a safe place to settle with a warm bed and food. They can have hope and be in the Kingdom of my Father.

So, My Child, where and how can you step out for the lost?... and, are you willing? I will step there with you. You are not alone. I will guide and protect you at all times.

DEEP WITHIN THE FOREST

We are walking into a deep forest, the trees are very tall. It is fairly open ground with some small brush and is easy walking. Birds are singing everywhere in the tree tops, flying from tree to tree to get a better view of whatever birds look for.

Chipmunks are scurrying up the trees; squirrels are checking us out for a morsel of food. We are walking on an open deer trail. We come upon a small grassy green meadow area. We sit quiety for a spell on the soft cool grass and listen, watch and observe our surroundings.

Open your eyes and look all around. What do you see? Look with my eyes; now what do you see?

I see trees of all shapes, colors, sizes and varieties. All are perfectly made. They serve as homes and food for the creatures that live within this forest. There is something here to meet all of their needs.

On the ground, there are bushes, vines and grasses of many varieties. Some serve as food, some as shelter and some a hiding place for the animals and birds. Insects are flying in the air, feeding on various vegetation. The grassy level provides for the smaller creatures and some of the flowers blooming here and there are intended for the insects to pollinate. Other special varieties are for the hummingbirds.

Several different types of wild berries are edible for mankind as well as beast. Even a little field mouse stops by to say his hello. I see God's handy work everywhere I look, even into the heavens. The sun provides daylight and nourishment for the plants and warmth for the creatures. Clouds cool down the heat of the day and bring forth the rains brings life support for all living things. Without the water there would be no life.

Yes, these are God's creations. We see his hand in every moment of time. God formed our world in thousands of years, His time. As human beings we admire it, we use it, but we also abuse it.

I'm sure it breaks God's heart when we misuse his creations.

Jesus, I see a tear falling on your face. It does on mine, too, when I think about man's misuse and destruction of such beauty that has taken eons of time to form. God is still creating. Just look up and around. We are still finding new planets, galaxies, plants, creatures of the deep sea and other living things.

Who says there is no God? He is everywhere. Just open your eyes and look around.

POWERS AND PRINCIPALITIES

Lord, show me why these days, these months seem to pass by so quickly. I know it takes me longer to get things done that I used to do quickly. I don't really feel that I am accomplishing anything on your behalf. I am just passing the hours away. I do your will in these last days?

The air is so full of the powers and principalities of the world. They are all around us.

Satan is pouring out every trick and action upon the people of the world. With disasters, sins of immorality are worldwide 24/7, everywhere you go; everywhere you look. Even the children don't know right from wrong. If it feels good, do it.

Life seems to be in fast-forward with no deadline, so we feel like we have to do everything fast – hurry, hurry, hurry. Live it up – as there may be no tomorrow – as we may be wiped out by terrorist attacks. We don't feel we have accomplished anything worthwhile. It is all at a standstill. Everything we do seems so unfinished.

I feel bombarded with things I need to do for the Kingdom, but I also feel there is a blockage. It seems to go nowhere. There is a heaviness and darkness all around me. Yet I feel internal peace and joy.

Lord, how can I feel both activities at the same time? Everything is spinning around me and I am just sitting here watching it all happen. I feel crushed. There's a pressure around me.

The sad part is that so many people have no clue of what is ahead and I'm not reaching them either. Many know, but do not believe; many do not want to know. So few really do know the truth.

Lord, touch our pastors in our churches, the ministers, the teachers, the prophets, the apostles and all who work to present the word... the truth of the word.

Lord, I am asking for our church to bring us back into the gospel songs, back into fire and brimstone ministry. That's what brought in the revivals in the past and it will do so again. People really hunger and thirst for real "down-to-earth" worship... worship that brings down the glory, the power and praising of the Lord. They want to sing real songs and worship with great spirit.

It isn't the good food, the internal activities or great preaching that will bring awakening. It is great, the true WORSHIP UNTO THE LORD. That's what brings in the glory.

If we go back to our roots, the church walls won't be able to contain all the people. Yes, they hunger and thirst for real down-to-earth WORSHIP that shakes the building and fills the altars where people pray, praise and fall on their faces when worshiping before the Lord. Bring down the angels, the glory of the Lord.

Let's stop playing church and pleasing man and please God instead. Praise Him, worship Him in truth and in Spirit. The church is crying out for this kind of worship. Our spirits are hungry!!

Ephesians 6:12

DESOLATE, FORGOTTEN

Here we are at the garden, now so desolate and neglected. The plants of last year lie dead and decaying. It makes me feel so sad; everything is waiting for someone to come along and clean away the old and make a way for the new to break forth.

When we look down close into the decaying vegetation, we can see new sprouts trying to break through. Some are bent over and pushing hard on the rubbish that is holding it down from above. Some are pale and whitish in color as the warm sun cannot reach it. Occasionally we can see a plant standing tall, trying to show its best side but, because it has been neglected, it is scrawny and weak. The garden patches that were once so beautiful and lush are all in such despair.

Lord, there is so very much to do here as it has been neglected for so very long, it almost looks hopeless.

Yes, My Child, these are the lost and forgotten. They are all around us, but everyone just walks on by in their own little world. Many of these people have cried out for help for someone to just stop and visit with them momentarily. They have lost their hope, so they lie in despair and neglect.

My Child, it is never too late; there is always hope and renewal. They just need someone to come by with love and a caring heart; stop by and talk with them, encourage and welcome them into your world.

Talk and teach them, nurture them, bring them into my Kingdom. Tell them how much God the Father loves them. Watch them grow and mature as you minister to their needs. Your love and words will quickly scatter among them and multiply. Once again they will be as beautiful roses, shining with the glory from above.

THE MIGHTY COLUMBIA RIVER

The river, big and wide and deep.
I often wonder how far or where did it originate?
Somewhere way off in a distant place,
Up high on a mountain top from melting snow.

The wind pushes the water to wash the river banks.
Churning, tumbling the rocks into pebbles,
which after hundreds of years turn into sand.
The waves have eroded the banks away,
Small trees have fallen victim at its mercy.

Ships pass by. I wonder where home port is?
Where are they headed? What is their cargo?
What is hidden in its hull?
Clothing, toys, furniture... all of the above?
It truly is a mystery.

Gentle ripples wash onto the shore
from the gentle wind.
A vapor trail in the blue sky above from an airplane.
How far has it come? Where is it going?
People anxious to arrive at their destiny.

The tides come and go.
Wonder what new things they bring
with each new tide?
The big boats moving with the changing tide.
The tugboats, little toot and big toot,
All have a place to be and a job to do.

Fishing boats are jogging around
for just the right location to catch that big one.

The big tall bridge... cars seem to never stop...
Crossing over, the big ships pass freely under.
I can see the cars on the highway across the river,
as they speed down the highway,
all having someplace to be.

The mountains with dark and light areas
Some have bare places logged off;
Other patches with tall evergreens.
The mountain tops look as though
they are manicured.
They chang over the horizon with ease
And interesting shapes and valleys, too.

All these things seem to be such a mystery
But we all know...
God is in charge and made all things

HELLO GOD. IT'S ME AGAIN

I'm so sorry I neglect spending more intimate time with you. Please forgive me. I know it is not good to be so busy doing Gods' work and not taking time to spend personal time with you. I sometime forget the importance of the intimate relationship with you personally. I keep asking for more of you, but am not giving you some of my time in return within my day.

Yes, I can name lots of excuses, but we both know that's what they are... excuses.

Our walks in the gardens are so very special. We are spending special time together. It's like Martha and Mary; one was busy serving, while the other was listening and learning and spending special intimate time with you.

Oh God, I love you so very much and I know you love me.

HEAVENLY GARDENS

Everywhere I look, everywhere I walk, the beauty is so magnificent. To my left are fields and fields of white lilies, all about the same height – waist high – swaying and nodding in the breeze. The fragrance is soft and pure.

To the right of me are rows and rows of purple lilacs. The air is filled with their fragrance. They too are swaying in the soft breeze, appearing to be waving and beckoning me to come closer.

In the center where we are standing, we are surrounded with red roses. The ground underneath the roses is covered with fragrant rose petals. I'm afraid to take a step as I will crush them.

This is the Trinity. I was sent by My Father to shed my blood upon the ground to save the people of the earth. That is represented by the red roses.

The white lilies denote My Father in Heaven. The purple lilacs represent the Holy Spirit.

The sweet scent you smell is the fragrance of the heavenly gardens that await you in Heaven.

Chapter Three

A WALK ON THE BEACH

Jesus and I are walking on the beach by the seashore. It is a calm and beautiful day with wispy clouds in the deep blue sky.

The waves are gentle with a swishing sound as they roll upon the sandy shore. You can see a squirt of water coming out of the sand as the water rushes over a clam that had been feeding there.

The water birds are running along the water's edge, searching for food. Seagulls come and go; many land and sit upon the water. They rise and fall with the wave movements. Some dive down to catch a small fish to eat while many just sit and relax and bob up and down.

It is so peaceful and tranquil here.

My Dear Child, the sea birds have no cares as they know there is plenty of food; they just need to put in some effort to search it out. They know they are safe from predators from above and have some protection from the deep water, but they also know they have to be alert for the creatures in the deep that sneak up from behind who are also searching for food – them.

You see, my people are like that. Those who trust, believe and follow and obey me have no fear, as they have me and my powers to fight against the enemy that tries to sneak in and overpower them.

I provide their protection and supply their needs as I do with the fowls of the air, land and sea.

For the birds, they learn from their parents what to watch out for and how to survive the elements. For my people, I have chosen you, but you have to accept me, hear and learn my commands or you will suffer the consequences when you don't.

The birds frequently lose their lives if they are not alert to the dangers. They don't get a second chance. But for you, through your salvation, I am with you always; even in the bad times. You have to believe, trust and follow my Word. You have everlasting life.

When the waters are calm, life is great and food is plentiful. The rough waters can mean life or death without my help and protection. You can become a lost soul.

Yes, the footprints are in the sand behind us.

James 3:4 Steered by a small rudder

THE MASTER'S GARDEN

Suddenly we are standing in the middle of a magnificent garden. There is every kind of food one could ever dream or imagine – from the smallest seed or fruit to the largest squash.

Fruit trees of every kind or type are so heavy, the branches are touching the ground. There are more than I have ever seen before and will ever see again until I get to Heaven.

There are all classes of people everywhere from every nation and color, from the very poorest to the very richest; from the nomads to the kings. Some are dressed in their finest royal robes; others are in torn rags.

When fruit is picked off a tree or plant, it just seems to replenish itself immediately as each one is taken away.

There is a commotion off in a distant corner. Someone is trying to collect money for the produce as the people leave, but there is a very tall guard ushering him off the premises.

As we walk through the gardens and among the people, I see the lame and crippled being helped. People are helping them to fill their baskets and carry them out for them; others stand around and watch, grumbling, as they speak against the helpers for fear they won't get their own fair share.

Lord, why are some so greedy and selfish? Can't they see there is an abundant amount for all?

My Child, those people are never happy or satisfied with the things I have given them. They expect and always want more, they feel they have earned it and society owes them. Others have done nothing to deserve it. They do not realize that it is they that have done nothing for mankind. They have always put themselves first. These lame and poor have always shared what little they may have with others who also have nothing. They are the blessed; they have sown seed; they are being served with blessings and with abundance for their giving to others.

If you look around, most people are helping others with their heavy loads and carrying their baskets for them, if needed. There are many ways of serving others; even the smallest of gifts never goes unnoticed. Many give with greed and selfishness in their hearts, but many more give from the love within. They serve with and receive my blessings. Giving something ever so small but with love is a blessing in itself.

SO SHALL YOU SOW,
SO SHALL YOU RECEIVE

DEAR JESUS

Please forgive us, Lord God, for we have sinned and forsaken you in all our ways. Forgive our nakedness, for we have shamed you with our corruptness. You made your words perfect and true; you made us in your image of perfection.

Then, along came that sly and crafty serpent that spoke sweet words in his canny way, "You will not surely die; God just doesn't want you to know good and evil, as you would be like Him."

So in our weakness and curiosity, we listened to his lies.

Now look at us today. We opened the doors to his tricks; we allowed our minds to take in our surroundings. Even though we were capable of choosing good or evil, we took the easy and fun route. Now we are corrupt and living in an immoral world.

Please forgive us, God, for our foolishness. I know your mercy and grace covers us all, but so few have accepted your love. As the straight and narrow road is pure and light, it is very difficult to walk without your guidance.

So many fall out of line and say, "It is just too difficult. I cannot do it. The rules are too strict."

They give up hope and don't receive your salvation.

I am what the Bible says I am.

I can do what the Bible says I can do.

CLIMBING THE MOUNTAIN

I fall, I stumble, I roll down that mountain to the valley below. I cry out your name, Jesus. You take me by the hand and help me back up the mountain side. Yes, one step at a time; slowly but surely, never letting go.

From the mountain top I see your glory shining brightly from the heavens above like a wash over the earth. I feel the mountain rumble with your great power; my legs tremble.

You raise your hand and flashes like lightning shoot through the air, brighter than the sun, as it lights the way to eternity.

You hold me in your hands; you light my way; you guide my steps from my enemies. You enable me to climb the highest mountain.

This is the awesomeness of my Lord and Savior. He is my strength, my all.

Habakkuk 3:1-3

GOD SPEAKS; THUNDER ROLLS

Do you hear His voice so loud and clear, calling?
Listen with you ears open and with your heart.
Listen as it thunders across the open waters.
Listen as it rumbles across the desert sands.
Listen as it rolls up the mountainside to the tops.
Do you hear?

Do you hear Him calling?
He stands on the mountain tops, flashing, flashing.
Flashing His glory down and over all the land and
     seas.
Flashing His light so clear and bright,
His glory as He watches over you and calls your
     names, one by one

He is covering you and the earth with His glory.
Yes, listen for His thundering voice.
It is calling unto you and me.
He is king and Lord over all the earth, big and small,
Mankind and every creature.
He is king and Lord over all creation.
He made everything upon and within the earth
Everything is wonderfully made

Psalm 29 NKJ

THE VOICE OF GOD

God of glory thunders and
is powerful and majestic.
Strikes with flashes of lightning.
Twists the oaks and breaks in pieces the cedars
Shakes the desert places.
Sits enthroned over the waters, enthroned as a king.
Blesses his people with Peace.

This is the voice of the Lord.

OUTSTRETCHED ARMS

I see the Lord in Heaven with outstretched arms hovering over our nation. He's calling us back into the Kingdom of God. He is hovering like a Father welcoming his child to run into his open arms, calling, calling, ***Come My Child that I may bless you with the things unseen that I have for you.***

He wants to embrace and gather in his sheep; rebuild and renew our land; trample down what the enemy has taken and torn apart.

There will again be dancing, singing, praises, worshiping and honoring the Lord God Almighty!

A new beginning – a new season. He is calling. He is waiting to bring our nation back to its foundations of *In God We Trust, Jehovah God*

THE VOICE OF THE LORD

Do you hear His voice so loud and clear... calling?
Listen with your heart and your ears open.
Listen as it thunders across the open waters.
Listen as it rumbles across the desert sands.
Listen as it rolls up the mountainside to the top.

Do you hear? Do you hear him calling?

He stands on the mountaintops, flashing, flashing.
Flashing His Glory down and over all the land and
seas.
Flashing His light so clear and bright... His Glory...
As He watches over you and calls your name.

One by one, He is covering you and the earth with His
Glory.
Yes. Listen for this thundering voice;
It is calling unto you and me.

He is King and Lord over all the earth...
Big and small, mankind and every creature.
He is King and Lord over all creation.
He made everything upon and within the earth.
Everything is wonderfully made.

Psalms 29   NKJ

TRAPS

How many times have we fallen into the traps –
those with gifts and promises of healings given
by prosperous prayer warriors and their Christian
ministries with offerings of ointments, prayer cloths,
Bibles, etc. – only to be conned into a large donation
to receive blessings and deliverance?

We fall into these traps because we are hungry for
the Word and in need of the blessing. We say and do
the things expected of us, but we never receive any of
that which has been promised.

When we do not study the Bible or know the Word
of God, we lose the game. The prayer warriors do not
live the Word of God. Paul did not heal and use his
anointing for money or the prosperity of mankind.
He was a man of God who preached and taught about
Jesus and his teachings.

When we study and learn, then we can ask Jesus
for knowledge and wisdom to be revealed to us at the
proper time and place.

He cannot manifest or recall his words if we have
not done our part and implanted the Word within our
spirit so it can be withdrawn.

Acts 19:6-12 NKJ

41

OVERWHELMING LOVE

Jesus takes my hand as we walk along the dry sandy beach. The waves are softly rolling on shore. Occasionally, a much larger wave comes ashore. The sea birds, large and small, search the wet sands for a morsel of food. The ocean's roar is gentle today as though talking to the winds. There is a ship way off in the distance. I wonder where it is headed or where has it come from... a land far away?

It is so quiet and peaceful; we don't say a word; we just walk.

His love becomes so overwhelming and I feel the power. I feel as though I am being carried in His arms. We are floating along as I feel no footsteps of my own.

The lesson here is that, no matter how heavy the burden seems, Jesus always is there to carry you through to the other side and lift you higher as He brings you into His loving arms.

STANDING ON SOLID GROUND

There is a meadow, lush green grass, soft as a bed of fluffy cotton, below outcroppings of rock and small hills with standing trees. Here we can see the earth washed away and a deep cleavage cut through to the base rock and washed clean from the heavy rains.

We are standing on sandy ground.

On the other side of the hill is a very deep, long and wide crack that looks like a bottomless pit. If one should fall into it, there would be no return. It looks like an earthquake fault promising everlasting death into the bowels of the earth. It's scary; the pit of Hell.

Over here there is a small plateau on one of the a rock outcroppings. It's standing on solid ground.

Now we are walking through a small grove of trees; some are small and others are very large, tall and straight. There are also some snags and broken and burnt ones.

They were struck by lightning – the voice and power of God. As the thunder rolls across the heavens, the earth will shake from the sound of his voice.

God is everywhere, all the time, even standing by your side through good and troublesome times.

Where are you standing?

Haggai 2:1-9 NKJ

GOD'S HELPING HANDS

I went to my eye doctor to get my glasses changed as my two year wait with the insurance was done and I was having trouble seeing.

The eye doctor started with his usual, "What do you see up there?"

One eye is about the same as before, but the other eye, nothing. I could not even see the first large "E" on the chart.

He grabbed his "deep-seeing-into-machine" and said I cannot see into your eye, I am sending you to the specialist at OHSU Casey Eye Clinic. Something in there is not right. We have a branch office of theirs here in Astoria now.

The doctor there could not see into my eye, either – even with her machines – so she called the main clinic in Portland and requested an appointment. I got one for two months later. (They are that busy!)

Now it is January and they have decided there must be an inner eye infection that an antibiotic shot should take care of. This is a quite common finding in people of any and all ages, even children, so it is not just an age-related thing. They do not know the cause.

So, I made an appointment in February for the injection and then waited for two months for it to do its job before having it rechecked. This time I was sent to the Longview, Washington Casey Clinic for the check-ups, but the weather was beginning to be a problem with traveling over mountain roads. The check-up showed no change, the problem was still there.

Their x-ray showed several bumps in the eye caused from the infection.

They then decided that surgery was the next step – a WHAT? – a Vitreous Macular Traction. The lining of the eye was messed up. The fluid was cloudy and it needed to be taken care of or I would lose the sight of that eye totally.

It is now late March and this has to be done in Portland at OHSU, which is the only place in Oregon where this procedure can be done.

According to the information sheet, "For a VMT, we remove the fluid that is in the eye now and replace it with sterile saline. The entire procedure takes one hour as it is a very slow process. We put you completely out for ten minutes while we insert one needle to extract the old fluid and another needle to inject the saline fluid and another needle with a tiny light so we can see what we are doing and not do damage to any other structures. In two to three weeks, nature replaces the saline with natural fluid.

"We don't understand how, but it happens. There will be a ten week wait for the next checkup and an x-ray to see if there has been a change and how much has healed..."

Now it is an every-two-month checkup until it is completely healed.

It's August now and it is almost healed. The bumps are gone and the lining of the eye is now smooth, but the lining itself has to grow back together as it has separated. They think another two months and it will be completely healed. Then I can get my glasses changed and everything should be AOK from then on.

I thank God for his helping hand and giving man the knowledge and science for saving my sight.

November 1st -- I am now completely healed although some scars remain.

THANK YOU, LORD

Thank you, Lord, for your food
that reminds me of your love.

SIN   Black represents my Sinful heart,
keeping me from you above.

BLOOD   Red represents the Blood you shed
to provide Salvation free.

CLEAN   White shows the Cleansing of my sin
as I put my faith in Thee.

HEAVEN   Yellow is for Heaven above;
my new home I will have someday.

GROWTH   Green is for the Growth
I will see as I read your Word and Pray.

ROYALTY   Purple shows You are King of All;
the one I choose to obey.

Thank you, Lord, for all this food,
it means more than words can say.

Chapter Four

MY VISIONS

Vision (according to Merriam-Webster Dictionary):
a: something seen in a dream, trance, or ecstasy; especially
a supernatural appearance that conveys a revelation

Throughout the remaining chapters of this book you will find stories defining some of the visions that I've had over recent years. For many of them, I am including interpretations of specific parts or symbols of these visions and how I believe that they relate to the Word of God and to my own life.

DOWN BY THE RIVERSIDE

I sit and watch the waves along the riverbank as they wash ashore. Some are gentle while others seem more aggressive. They all wash and cleanse the shoreline from other storms that have brought in debris that clutter the land.

Some seem to come far from shore and more vigorous. The washing of the waves on the shore is like the washing of my blood, removing my sins and cleansing my soul.

Some sins go deep that's why they come from such a far distance to cleanse and wash the shores.

We all have sinned and come short of the mark. Repent and ask God for forgiveness.

A VISION:
NEW CREATION

In my vision, I saw two small mounds of dirt... one on each side of my feet. They were about 18-20 inches high and the same across.

I was standing on the edge of a forest and the sun was shining brightly on the mounds and all around me, like a sunbeam. The sky was overcast with clouds, but I was standing in a tube of sunshine. There were no shadows. Everything was sharp and bright.

The mounds were beautiful and looked as though they may have been stumps at one time. They were covered with beautiful, lush green moss like the kind you fmd on fallen trees and growing under trees in the shady areas where the sun shines through occasionally.

There were also a few blades of green grass and a few white, silvery plants of lichen growing on them. There was a small outcropping of wood on one side of each mound. They were very clean; no tree debris, twigs... nothing... They were clean and pure.

On the very top of these mounds were active, healthy insects including small white worms, caterpillars and small centipedes. They were all very lively and quickly moving around and over each other as though they were finding and feeding on some kind of food. All were working together as one unit. They all looked like newborns or very young.

Although I don't like insects, I was fascinated and spellbound as I watched them. I was amazed by how clean everything was, especially here by the woods with all sorts of debris under the trees and falling from them continually.

Then, I heard, *This is new life, a new beginning, a change is coming*.

Does this mean God is moving me up into a new realm of ministry?

~~~~~~~~~

My interpretations of this vision's symbols:

Caterpillar – signifies the ability to change into greater potential

Worm – transformation, changing, more fertile

Sunlight – signifies creative energy and spiritual enlightenment

Grass grass – signifies new ideas and a fresh spiritual awareness

Wood – signifies spiritual good

Brown – signifies earth and fertility

Moss – signifies growth, end of a season

Forest – signifies entering new areas, understanding secrets of the spiritual world

Lichens – signifies purity, righteousness, redemption, honor, age

Green – signifies prosperity, growth, nourishment

Sun – signifies achieving success, intellect, awareness, unveiled vitality, energy

A VISION:
FLOWING WATERS

A wall of raindrops fall over the doorway. They are large drops; a heavy rain.

I didn't want to walk through the door into the rain as I didn't want to get wet. That water was cold!

I could hear people, but could only see them in a blur through the downpour. Others went through the door as I hesitated.

I finally walked through it and, to my surprise, I DID NOT get one drop of water on me.

It was pouring down. There was no way that I could not have gotten wet, but I didn't!

Wow!!

~~~~~~~~~~

My interpretations of this vision's symbols:

Rain – refreshment, release and new life, blessings
Water – purity, fertility, transition, wisdom
Stream – flowing, teaching spiritual doctrine

THE ELECT

My Dear Child, *these times are upon you.*
On these last days, the doors are opening.
I will be pouring out my spirit upon all those
that are open and willing to receive. Obey my
voice these last days. I will open blind eyes and
deaf ears with my glory and the workings of
many miracles; these will be common within the
churches.

Listen for my voice, obey my instructions for
you will walk in my steps for the world to see.

These are the latter rains. Only the elected
will be used in mighty ways.

Oh Lord, what do you mean "only the elect?" Do
you mean to be separated from the rest of us?

Yes, we all have a choice and many desire
to be used for your glory in these last days and
some don't.

Oh! I see. Some are workers; some are warriors;
some ministers and teachers; some intercessors.
These will be standing behind the miracle workers
and bringing in the harvest.

Thank you Lord.

A VISION:
PAILS OF WATER

There were empty buckets everywhere. I was to fill these pails with water and set them down outside and someone would take care of them from there.

The empty pails seemed to never stop coming. As soon as I would touch the handle of one pail, it was instantly filled with water. Someone would grab it and set it down as I grabbed another empty one.

I could hardly grab them fast enough as they just kept coming and coming. It was just ordinary water like we drink, BUT I noticed as they were set down that the water turned crystal clear and pure like nothing we have here on Earth.

There was a man at the other end picking up the pails of water and leaving with them.

I asked God what all those pails of water meant.

With your school lessons you have been praying and repenting of things as you have been lead. The many pails of water are the things you have been delivered of. The crystal clear pure water is the cleansing. I am the person on the other end, picking up the pails of water and walking away.

A VISION:
THE RIVER CROSSING

I was trying to get across the river. It was very wide and very deep; in fact, it was the Columbia River.

There were no boats or ferries available and no bridge, but I was supposed to go to the other side and minister to someone. Suddenly an eight-foot-wide bridge appeared. It was about 10 feet above the water with a very high wall on one side to hold back any strong winds so you wouldn't fall or get thrown in the water.

There were many people walking upon this bridge and someone on the other side needed my help.

I was terrified of the water. Suddenly there appeared a man who took my hand to walk me across the bridge. He guided and comforted me all the way.

When across, he pointed out the house where I was to go, then he was gone.

Inside was an elderly lady who was no longer able to get around. She was handicapped and very lonely. She needed direction as to where and how to get herself some needed physical help.

I was able to help her get the things she needed and make life easier for her.

HELPING HANDS

I had a luncheon date with my typist friend to exchange some papers that needed typed... We had a good visit and lunch but, when returning to my car, I found a flat, flat tire. I pulled the car around to the other side of the parking lot where there was lots of room to remove the tire. I stood by the car waiting for a nice younger gentleman to come along that I felt could help with my tire.

Several older seniors came by, then a car full of nice looking younger men stopped beside me. I asked if they would put my donut tire on my car for me as I was too far from the tire shop to drive there.

They agreed to do it, and three of them went to work while the young ladies waited. In no time, they had everything done and back in its place.

The tire shop couldn't find any cause for the flat, so put it back on after putting in a new valve and resealing the tire.

The next morning it was flat again, so back I went. They still couldn't fmd any reason for the flat.

The next day it was flatter than ever. I got enough air in to get to the tire shop once again. This time I reminded them that this was the third time. I suggested that they check the tread in the center of the tire and they would fmd a nice shiny nail head.

This time they did and, sure enough, there it was... a one-inch-long nail. It hadn't come through enough for them to feel it inside the tire and the hole was not large enough to blow bubbles in the water test.

So, all would be fixed and ready to go, I thought. But, again, they came back in and said they could not put the tire back on my car because it was bald.

I was told to continue to drive on the donut until I could buy two new tires. I replied, "My tires are just fine and they have plenty of tread on them yet.

So, he took me by the hand and told me to look at the front tires. They looked great, lots of tread.

Then, he turned the wheel and said, "Now look again. What do you see?"

I saw a very bald center with the cords showing. "Wow!"

"You need two new tires."

"Well, ok."

I then asked them to rotate the tires and check the brakes while they had everything off.

Again, he came out and asked me to take a walk with him. He spun the front one.

Fine. It rolled good.

Then we went around to the other side and he tried to spin it... only it did not spin.

"You have a brake that is dragging and it could freeze up. You need a brake job,, and the sooner the better. You also have a left broken bracket on your stabilizer bar but that can wait. It is important, but it won't affect your driving or cause an accident."

Well, when he got through with all of his "ands," it added up to over a thousand dollars, all of which I did not have.

Well, all in all, we worked out a schedule to get the emergency stuff done as quickly as possible. By waiting until after the first of the month, which wasn't too far away, we got the main stuff done for the time-being.

Again, God had his hand on me. The flat tire led to my getting the needed new tire which led to getting the dangerous accident-things taken care of without a mishap beforehand.

I shutter to think what could have happened if that tire had blown while I was driving or if the brakes had locked up.

Wow! God is so good! He really is protecting me!

BY THE SEASHORE

Jesus and I are again walking on the beach. It is a calm, quiet and serene afternoon, warm with a very slight breeze. I can see for miles in both directions. The water's edge is gently flowing, Waves are rolling upon the sandy beach.

Seabirds are swooping down to catch a small fish. Little sandpipers are busy running back and forth in unison like they do; when one turns, they all turn. They seem to always be in a hurry, ready to snatch that tiny morsel before others do.

The beach is clean as though the winds and water have washed it clean. No debris can be seen anywhere; not even logs thrown on shore by the storms.

Off in the distance, one can see the grasses where the shorebirds nest and there is a tree here and there. It is just Jesus and me.

I look back and see our footsteps together. As I wander, yours are there with mine, just as you will never leave or forsake me.

We talk about the things hidden deep within the ocean – the very biggest to the very smallest – the beautiful fishes and plants, each having their own species and purposes and character. We discuss their diets; the kinds of food they eat and the scavengers that keep the waters cleaned out of decay. These species are so efficient in their share of the housekeeping.

I am in awe and amazement at all the beauty and grace surrounding us. Each and every creature was created by your hand, and as you spoke the word to each individual, just as you did with each of us, all were perfectly made.

"If the big whale that swallowed Jonah were a real whale, it would have eaten him. He disobeyed me. I had to get his attention. I got it.

"'I am that I am.'"

Thank you Jesus for taking time to walk with me.I so enjoy our time together.

THE RIVER WALK

As we walk along the riverbank, we meet and see other people. Some just walk for the exercise; some for the joy of the Lord's creations; others to visit with passersby.

Many birds are flying overhead, each with their own mission. Some just soar with the winds above; some talk to each other, similar to those visiting below.

We stop for a moment and just listen to the birds and watch the water which is heading for the nearby ocean as it gently rolls up the bank, rolling pebbles as it returns.

We look across the river's wide expanse. A few white caps from the winds rise across the water. Some small fishing boats drift along with the tide, dragging their nets behind them. Many catch fish for the local markets, while some just fish for pleasure and their own food.

Occasionally, a large ship passes by on its way to the ocean – barges, log carriers, grain ships and, oh yes! Here comes a car carrier. Each has its own special cargo. Some are delivering cargo from other countries; some are empty and arrive to fill their ships and return to their homeland.

A sea lion pops his head above the water now and then. They devour a lot of our food fish, especially the salmon. But, God has provided food for mankind as well as the creatures of the sea and land.

This walk provides a way to enjoy each others company, spending time together – a special time. It enables us to enjoy God's creations and breathe in the fresh air.

He has provided these things for us. His creations enable us to not only survive, but enjoy the beauty and peace that surround us, Everything comes from the Father in Heaven.

It is overcast outside, but still a warm summer day. I feel a rain drop, but that, too, is part of God's plan. The rains replenish the earth, give us life's sustaining water and bring food from the stream beds to feed the fish. The storms stir the seas.

Water is a life-line to all living things. What a wonderful God we serve.

LIFE-SAVING DOCTOR'S APPOINTMENT

Last Thursday my husband, Fred, went in for a check-up with the doctor. When the nurse took his vitals, they found that his pulse was slower than it should be, so they did an EKG and found his heart rate was down to 25-28. Normal heart rate is 60-90, so they called me to come get him and take him to the emergency room at our local hospital if I could. Otherwise, they would call an ambulance to take him as he could not drive himself.

Well, knowing my husband, he was probably irate and telling the doctors a thing or two. Sure enough, that is what he was doing when I got there.

He told the doctor. "I drove myself over here at 55 mph and I can drive myself to the hospital."

He headed for his truck, arguing every step of the way. The doctor was right on his heels, telling him that if he got into his truck instead of my car, he would call the police.

Well, as you have guessed by now, I took him, and he grumbled all the way there. They put him right into an examination room. I had copies of the EKG tapes for them to see what was going on.

They got him hooked up to all their machines and his heart rate dropped down to 20.

I could see it; he couldn't. They immediately got on the phone to make arrangements to get him to a hospital in Portland, about 200 miles away, and into surgery to install a pacemaker.

An ambulance came and off they went to the Portland hospital. Enroute, the ambulance attendant told the doctors at the Portland hospital that Fred's heart rate had dropped to 17.

Well, it was obvious that he was on his way out to see the Lord, but they made it to the hospital and he was stabilized until the next morning when they performed the surgery.

His doctors wouldn't allow him to move. They had tubes and stuff everywhere they could put stuff, he said, and they were all amazed that he never fainted or went out totally.

His pulse was stable and the new pacemaker was keeping things moving at his normal rate. Because he never blacked out, they allowed him to walk as he felt he was able to. When he was released, they brought him home by ambulance. He did quite well, but didn't want to follow doctors' orders.

He was a person who had never followed doctors' orders for anything, even when he had a massive heart attack.

A VISION:
SLIDING DOORS

I am sitting in a restaurant eating dinner when suddenly I found myself standing in front of two huge sliding doors that had opened wide onto a vast field of green grass. It was a lush, manicured lawn that had beautifully pruned and manicured shrubs and small, trimmed trees growing there. It looked as though it may be a garden or memorial of some kind.

I could see the small birds and butterflies as they flew in and around the plants. It was very quiet and serene, almost like a cemetery, but there were no headstones.

I stepped back inside the building and just stood there wondering what I was to do or where I was to go. I was profoundly engrossed with the vastness and beauty of what I had seen.

I asked God what was He trying to show and tell me. I heard, *Disciple, Teach New Converts*.

~~~~~~~~~

My Interpretations of this vision's symbols:

Serene – completely at peace, calm
Grass – spiritual awareness
Green – divine activity
Cemetery – spiritual regeneration, seek higher knowledge
Quiet – listen more deeply to anticipate
Fields – renew, consider your chosen field, harvest opportunity, further self spirituality
Memorial – memory to move on, tangible representation
Doors – entry into new phase of life and opportunities

A VISION:
THE WHIRLPOOL

My husband and I were out for a drive. We stopped at a park near the mouth of the Columbia River. We could see the bar and the waves. It was a clear and warm day and there was a big house near the shore off in the distance.

We got out of the car and went for a walk down the beach, Once on the beach, we went in different directions.

I was standing watching the waves as they came ashore and listening to the sounds around me, when suddenly several cars came in at once into the parking lot behind me.

A group of people gathered as though having a meeting of some kind. As I continued to watch the water and sea birds, a small whirlpool appeared. Soon it turned turbulent and became larger, forming a large black hole – a huge water whorl. It was an amazing site, and I got very excited.

I pointed to it and yelled at the group of people so they too could see it, too. A couple turned to look, but went back to their conversation with the group, uninterested. As I watched it go back down into calm water again I continued standing there, not believing what I had just seen.

At once, another one began to form and it was bigger than the first. It moved my spirit so strongly that I began to cry. I wanted my husband to see this once-in-a-lifetime spectacle, but by this time, the crowd of people had gone and my husband was almost back to the car, but still too far away to see any of it.

I saw this as a warning. To me, it signified that there is trouble coming, but we will not be harmed or become a part of it, as there is a hedge of protection around us.

~~~~~~~~~~

My Interpretations of this story's symbols:

Whirlpool – depressed center tending to drag down; the state of nations in turmoil
Whorl – circle, around

I have a deep burning, grieving in my spirit.

- It is for my nation, for the things that are coming upon us soon.
- For Israel, her protection, and it "will not be divided'
- For our church; for the Holy Spirit to fall upon us and deliver us and bring us into the will of God.

We must intercede for these things.

Chapter Five

BUYING THE FARM

I was very sick for a couple weeks during the Christmas holidays several years ago, so I went to the ER for some help. It was a lung virus. The doctor said it was so new they didn't have a name for it yet. It was just me who suffered with it – two other friends came down with it about the same time that I did. None of us had seen each other for a couple of weeks before we got sick, so we didn't catch it from one another.

I have been sick with other things that float around, but this was worse than anything I had experienced. In fact, I was coughing so hard, I really thought I wasn't going to make it. I felt that I was going to buy the farm this time.

I coughed so hard and so much that I tore something in my stomach and couldn't eat. My doctor gave me something to stop the bleeding and heal what ever was wrong. That took over a month before I could eat anything other than soft food and very little. I lost a lot of weight in the process.

My husband took good care of me and the church was praying that he would not get this awful bug also. Praise God, he didn't. God does answer prayers.

Skipper, our cat, knew something was very wrong as our daily routine was completely off schedule. He wouldn't even go outside; he just stayed indoors and close to each of us.

In total, I was sick for over a month with it.

GOD IS IN CHARGE

Well, here I go again. They did a biopsy on February 3, 2015. After five trips to the emergency room, trying to stop the bleeding, they prepared me for emergency surgery.

In the meantime I completely fell apart emotionally. I called my pastor as soon as they informed me that we were going into surgery, but soon after talking to him, I felt completely at peace and all the fear left me. I knew God was with me and was in charge.

On February 5, at midnight, they performed a mastectomy, removing my left breast.

They sent me home twelve hours later. Usually, following surgery, they send people at my age to a care center for a few days before allowing them to return home. But, the doctors and hospital declared me a miracle, as I had no pain and no meds.

The hospital's social services coordinator called my church to set up home meals and any other type of help I needed until our daughter could get to Astoria. At the time, she was in Colorado where her husband's mother had died and where he was needed to settle the estate.

On February 9, they returned home to Eugene, Oregon, but both have very bad colds. Alice was able to arrive on Saturday, February 14 and was kept very busy running me back and forth to doctors' appointments.

Yes, it was cancer but it was localized. They did other tests to determine if it had spread to other areas, but it had not.

God was in charge. I feel there was a reason why I went through this. I do not blame God for this situation. We were praying for healing, but as I said, God is in charge. I trust his directions.

I continued to do great – no pain, no redness, no weeping of the wound. Everything healed as it should. It was a miracle.

I praise God and honor him.

GOD DOES ANSWER PRAYER. I KNOW!!

God is in Charge - Update

What I am so very grateful for is God never allowed me to think about what "could be." It could have been all throughout my entire body as I had put off seeing the doctor for over a year. It turned black and I decided that I had better do something. Because I was so positive that God was going to heal it, I refused to seek outside help.

There were many people praying for my healing and God was healing me. Despite the delay in treating it, the Stage Three cancer did not spread. It was contained within the breast. Praise God!

My daughter Alice had come to help me for two weeks following my surgery. When she arrived back home, she went in for her own long-overdue mammogram. Ironically, they found two lumps in her breast. The biopsy showed Stage One cancer in one lump and she immediately underwent treatment. She, too, had a miracle healing. Praise God!

God doesn't always answer in the way we think or want, but he does answer. I praise and thank Him every day.

Psalm 23

THE BOARDWALK

As we walk along the boardwalk, beside the river's edge, we pass many other people walking too. They are enjoying the warm sunny day, watching the shoreline birds as they swoop down over the water.

Children are playing and running to and fro, chasing each other and trying to catch butterflies.

Some adults stop in silence and just gaze at the river, watching the ripples of tide as it flows out toward the ocean. Many faces are shining with the brightness of the sun, but beneath it all one can sometimes see the pain and sorrow.

Others walk by, laughing with joy in their voices and upon their faces. Someone is pushing a wheelchair with an elderly person, and close behind is a wheelchair with a child in it. One wonders why and what brought them to this place in their life.

The child is laughing while the adult just looks around with sadness.

There must be a passenger ship ashore as there are many people of foreign nations, many walks of life enjoying the activity on the boardwalk. They all seem to marvel at the scenery and tranquility of their surroundings and the beauty of the landscape.

I show you these things to see the reaction of the many different people. No two are the same and each see and respond differently to the same environment. I made each and every person's personality different, but they all possess the same spirit and a choice of how they may choose to direct it. I made them all in my image on the inside; they each just look different on the outside covering.

These are all my creations. I know each and every one intimately. Here are the rich and the poor; the famous, the unknown and the forgotten. All come together in one accord; no one is looking upon another with despair or horror. Everyone is an individual, accepting others just as they are and who they are. No one is looking for fault or the color of their skin.

They are all my people. All nations come together in one place at one time, enjoying the beauty I have created. Soon they all will return to their homelands and back to their lifestyle and the things of the world around them.

Some are struggling but surviving; some will continue in their life of pleasure; and some will return to their love of serving me.

A MIRACLE

Because of my continuing eating and stomach problems, the doctors ordered more x-rays and CT scans for me. I was having difficulty eating and getting food into my stomach.

The x-rays showed that when I had the lung virus in December, I had the dry heaves that caused the stomach to react violently. In the past, I had a mild hiatal hernia that allowed me to only eat small amounts at a time. Since the pressure was so heavy against my lungs, I had trouble breathing and could hardly walk across the room. That's when I started losing weight and as the problem worsened the weight loss continued.

The intense deep coughing with the lung virus made my stomach problem much worse and it caused bleeding in my stomach.

This time, the x-ray showed I no longer had the hiatal hernia and the stomach opening was clear and healed. The doctor gave me meds to heal and stop the bleeding in my stomach.

Now I am eating much better.

What happened to the hernia? We know God does make good things from bad things sometimes. Did it go back into place when the stomach was in violent action?

Medical knowledge says this can't be. We know, that, that with God, anything is possible.

I had good Christian doctors and nurses. God does answer prayers, not always the way we want. I didn't receive a major miracle physical healing as we were praying, but God did heal the rest of my body. It's free of cancer and He gave me other miracle evidence throughout my recovery. I am a walking and talking testimony.

I praise God for this miracle and give him all the credit.

COME WALK WITH ME

Do you hear the groans of the earth? It moves ever so slowly, very quietly, as we burden it with monumental, towering concrete buildings, skyscrapers and colossal bridges.The weight is so overbearing; even the rocks are crying out.

Do you hear the trees in the forest whispering? – wondering what is next? They hear the humming of the chair saws off in the distance as the falling trees echo through the forest, coming closer every day, one tree at a time. My beautiful rain forests, are being taken away.

The little stream, quietly but swiftly flowing through the woods once provided watering holes for the animals, great fishing holes and shallow, calm pools where one could cool one's feet while children played.

Now it is just a trickle in places, trapping the little fish. It's no longer a babbling brook teaming with life and serenity.

This was part of the world that God made so perfect; one that offered and gave everything to man that he would ever need or desire to survive. It provided comfort, food and refuge – food to nourish our bodies; herbs to season our food and heal our bodies. He created all of this for man and beast.

What happened Lord? In some areas. we have preserved, cared for and maintained your precious creation. In many cases we have changed your creation to our liking and pleasures; completely destroying areas with our chemicals and waste.

Forgive us, Lord, for our thoughtlessness, lack of caring and ingratitude.

What have we done Lord?

MY DEAR CHILD

In these last days I will use you mightly. You have come so far. You have grown in strength and closer to me. You have learned much in these past months. You have looked upon and praised me. You walked through the fire. You continued to praise me with every step. You are a witness to those around you and you humbled yourself in my glory. You walked in peace and without fear.

I look around me and I see many who also walked through these steps and they were hurt and very afraid and had many troubled times, they suffered much. I feel so blessed, but yet I feel so guilty because of their pain and struggles and I was so pain-free and blessed and healed.

WALKING THROUGH THE FIRE

Oh, My Dear Sweet Child, I feel your pain and your dismay. I am with you always. You are standing in the fiery furnace as the three brothers, Shadrack, Meshack and Abendego did; but I too am standing there with you and holding you. You will withstand these flames of fire for soon the flames will cease and a new door will open wide. You will walk in glory and honor as I will present you to my people, the church, and they will listen to what you have to say to them, for my sake and my glory will abound in you.

(I was having a pity party and God was listening in)

REST IN PEACE

I have complete rest and peace. God has everything
in His control. You have answered my prayers even
though it wasn't the way I had hoped or expected
it to be. In your own way, time and will, you did
answer, only in a different way. I never gave up hope
or faith. I knew you would answer. I knew with my
whole being that you would heal me. I stood firm
and witnessed to all I met. "God is in charge." Some
would agree, while others would give me that look
and walk away.

RETREAT AT CANNON BEACH

Our retreat was awesome as usual. I did not ask for anything for myself this time. I was totally devoted to my friend who accompanied me. I wanted to ensure that she received everything God had for her. It was her divine appointment.

While there, she received release in the movement of her right arm, allowing it to lift up completely. It had gotten that way as a result of a previous surgery.

She can walk better and straighter now. God will also.give her complete healing for her brain for the damage the strokes have done. God is still working, He is in charge.

I too received healing and can raise my arm up following my own surgery which severed some major nerves. The upper one is totally healed and it moves freely with no pain or numbness. The lower one is still very tender, but God is healing that one also.

I also had sciatica and my back is healed from pain.

The past week, I have been told from four different people that they can see POWER around me.

Wow! I feel different. I feel as though I am walking on air, about a foot above the ground and totally different spiritually. WOW! I can't explain how or why.

I am able to worship deeper than I have ever done before.

DANCING FLAMES

There are dancing flames of fire all around you; flames of my glory and flames of power and peace. My Child, the flames are dancing all around you, for with a servant's heart, they burn away all – yes, all – things that are not of me and impure.

They bring my love, joy and peace within to those around you. Yes, they can feel and see my power and my glory. Yes, power and glory, as you walk by them, as they saw and felt my glory on Moses. These flames dance all around and over people as they did on Pentecost. You are the burning bush as you speak to my hurting people; as the purifying fire touches and speaks to their spirits.

HIGH ON THE MOUNTAIN TOP

We are sitting on the bench in the garden by the pool. The soft fragrance of the flowers fill the air. The sky is filled with clouds. Some gray ones are moving quite fast while others – large, billowing white clouds seem to move with an inner energy – almost in jubilance.

There are some areas of deep blue sky and a slight breeze. The birds are singing and some are busily carrying twigs for nest building.

As we sit and watch the clouds, they continually move to new places, donning new shapes and colors. Sometimes the sun is slowly covered by a darkened cloud and the sky becomes darkened, the air chilly.

As we wait and watch, everything changes totally again and again.

Jesus breaks the silence by saying, "My Child, as the clouds move around and change, no two are alike. Such is life. Every minute is different, every hour changes, every day is a new day, a new beginning.

The dark days are when you are at the foot of the mountain. Suddenly, the sky opens a new door, the sun shines brightly and you rush to the mountain top.

On the dark days, you feel sad and lonely; your load seems much too heavy. My words come into your mind and you begin thinking and speaking my words. That's when the sun comes out again. I hold you in my arms and together we climb back up the mountainside to the top.

My Child, there are so many of my people that don't know my words, so I can't come into their minds and carry them up the mountain. They just lie there, crippled in the darkness of the day.

If you gaze upon these flowers and can't see their inner beauty, you are not seeing with my eyes and my heart.

The fields are ready for harvest now. Spread the gospel to the broken-hearted that they too may see my glory and await my coming on the mountain top.

1 Cor. 3: 5-17 NKJV

A VISION:
THE KING OF GLORY

I see fields of roses; many, many roses of all colors and varieties formed in groups of perfect rows of color as a rainbow. Their perfume fills the air.

The sky above is clear and deep blue with no clouds in sight. The breezes are gentle. There is perfect peace and serenity.

Butterflies flash their iridescent colors as they fly from flower to flower. The birds are singing their songs as angels do in their heavenly choir above.

You, Lord, are hovering over your fields of flowers with outstretched arms, admiring and leading your choir. Your rays of glory radiate from your fingers over the fields of glorious color below in rhythm with the songbirds.

As your glory brightens, the heavenly perfume magnifies and rises over and above the roses as a cloud. The perfume is intoxicating as it drifts over me.

Oh! how God brings blessings to us in so many ways. He lifts us up from our deepest times of sorrows and despair.

God is so good. He is in charge at all times, in all ways, even when we don't feel His presence and we think he isn't hearing our cries. Thank you, Jesus.

MY DEAR JESUS

I am so sorry I am having another pity party. I know you always make something good from bad things.

You have shown that to me many times, but especially most recently by having my daughter go have a physical, which in turn saved her life as they found her cancer in the very early stages.

Through her experience, she too is finding how to know you personally, not just know about you.

God is in charge. I know you don't give us more than we can handle. I also know you are with me every step of my journey, even through the times it seems there is no light at the end of the tunnel.

I also know there is victory ahead and you are standing there with outstretched arms, waiting for me to call your name.

So Lord, I am asking for faith, where I lack faith and strength and am weak. I know all these things will pass away. I ask myself many times, why do I still praise and worship you, even when I am so down and feel so lost? My answer is that I know you are with me and you will carry me through this ordeal as you have many times before.

Then I remember Job and all the things Satan put him through, yet he still praised and worshiped God. His victory in the end of his ordeal was greater than anything he could imagine or have had before.

My Child my dear sweet child, you never lost sight of me or your faith. You continued to praise and worship me even in your darkest hours. You are witnessing to all those around you in my name. It encourages them to seek my face, as they see my glory in yours.

A VISION:
CLIMB THAT MOUNTAIN

As I sit in the valley, the light is dim as shadows move around the mountain top. I can see the top, but it looks so far away. There is a light shining from it as brightly as a beacon of a lighthouse.

I don't have the strength to climb back up, even though it has a wide clear path. I feel such sorrow for the things around me. I just sit here and weep. No, no! I'm not having a pity party. I am crying because of all the saddened people I see around me.

Some are walking as if in a stupor; some are just sitting and holding a pet; some are just standing and crying.

So many are suffering as the devastation lies all around as far as you can see. They have no hope, no possessions, nothing. Everything they dreamed of, strived for and worked for is gone. So much pain and sorrow.

Oh God, how much longer must these people have to suffer? Many have nothing to hope for while others know, even so, there is a future and they have to keep their eyes upon the Lord, for you are their future, their hope and their strength.

Lord, I am asking you to give them all the faith, strength and hope that they need to get through this, It is faith that they lack.

As we join hands and climb back up that mountainside together, we must know that we will find victory against all things that come against us,

YOU ARE OUR STRENGTH AND HOPE. Thank you Lord.

THE STILL SMALL VOICE

Many times I feel I'm not really doing much. I need to do more meaningful things to serve God. I have a few in-home seniors I visit once a week on a regular basis. Mostly we just visit and talk about their daily lives and needs and, usually, along God comes into the conversation.

Many times, I have experienced going and visiting one of them spontaneously, with no plan to see them on a particular day. Usually, I had had a very strong feeling that I needed to go there even though I personally had other things to do on that day, but a small voice told me that I was needed there.

Sometimes it is the direction of my spirit that alters my route on that day. When I arrive, frequently I would find that person in a deep depression because of something that had come up in their daily living. It may have been personal, an illness or a close family member that has caused them concern.

The first thing they say is, "I am so glad you came, I was praying to God desperately for you to come. I need someone to talk to and pray with me.

Many times we ask God to tell us what He wants us to do and how we are to serve Him. Many times He tells us when we least expect it without knowing it is coming from him – not realizing and we are hearing and obeying His still small voice.

What a blessing when things turn out great.

Listen and obey that still small voice. Be ready whenever it comes and take that first step out in obedience and watch what happens.

Then he said to his disciples, the harvest truly is plentiful, but the laborers are few, therefore pray the Lord of the harvest to send out laborers into His harvest.

Matthew 9:37,38 NKJV

FEAR AND ANXIETY

One day, I left to make my weekly visits to my homebound ladies. The blind lady was first. She was really down physically, mentally and spiritually. She is elderly and has many physical ailments. That visit was a short one this time as she just wasn't up to visitors.

I then went on to see my other lady, Karen, but I knew that I was running short on time. I had a 2:00 p.m. appointment that was important to keep, I had an hour, though, so I figured that she would understand if I didn't stay as long as I usually do. But, I thought to myself, "Maybe I should just wait until Monday when I can stay longer."

I decided to go anyway. As I walked through the door, she met me in her wheelchair, in tears. She had just received a telephone call telling her that her daughter, Sherry, was very ill and had just been taken by ambulance to the hospital. Sherry was experiencing heart problems and Karen had no way of traveling the 20 miles to the hospital to be by her side in her time of trouble. She was extremely upset about the situation.

I went inside and sat down and listened to her carrying on about no one offering to take the time to help her get to Sherry as her own car was disabled at the time. I continued to sit there and just listen and watch her go on and on about the fact that her caretaker would not take her as she didn't have the time.

She began to get very upset and very angry and as she went into a rage, she became completely out of control. The caretaker and I just watched and listened.

I could see something needed to be done. Things began flashing through my mind. How could I put a stop to this anxiety attack without making it worse or causing a bigger scene? I got up out of my chair and stood right in front of her, leaned over her and began shaking my finger in her face.

"Now wait a minute," flashed through my mind. "What am I supposed to do or say now that I'm here? You don't shake your finger at an adult... a young child, maybe, but not an adult without asking for a smack in the face."

I told Karen very firmly, "You need to calm down and take control of your thoughts."

Then I told her to take a deep breath and say, "God is in charge." I repeated these statements several times as she continued to rattle on.

Finally she stopped and looked at me and said, "No, I don't want to say that."

I just kept repeating "God is in charge."

Finally, grudgingly, she said it. I kept repeating it until she herself could say it from her heart.

She then began to calm down and relax and began repeating it over and over. One could see the physical, mental, and spiritual change as it progressed over and throughout her body.

She finally got control of her emotions and called her granddaughter and together they went to the hospital to see Sherry. She had gone into a diabetic coma and was hospitalized for a few days before going home.

Karen's young caregiver was frightened over the whole issue from start to finish and was afraid of me as I had confronted the issue. When it was all over, all she could say was, "Wow!" as she headed home.

I called Karen the next day. She had much joy in her and said she couldn't stop saying, "God is in charge," all the rest of the day until bed and started again through the next morning when she arose. She was still repeating it until my telephone call to her at 8:00 p.m. that following day.

ATTITUDE, APTITUDE

As we, Jesus and I, walk the aisles of my church, he shows me the hearts of those who are worshipping there. I see much physical pain, but there is also a sparkle in their eyes and joy on the faces as they praise the Lord.

I see sorrow upon a young mother's face. She is struggling to maintain a livelihood for her family and she is asking, "God, where are you? I am weak in faith and strength asking for your help Lord."

I see others glowing with your glory, their spirits jump with joy; their faces are aglow with your peace and love as they worship.

Here is one with fear and doubt; a very unhappy soul, carrying many past hurts, with disbelief and doubt of the things and people that surround him. He is overcome with physical and emotional pain, but refuses any help offered to him, fearing that those offering it may want something in return.

Many are standing with arms raised, rejoicing and praising God, worshiping with their whole beings, while others are only going through the motions so as not to be left out of the moment. One wonders why they came.

Then there is the couple – loners – sitting in the back, just observing, but listening and absorbing every word. You can see the word is touching their hearts, calling unto them.

There is the talkative one. She wants everyone to know what she is doing to serve God and also letting us know what we should be doing, as church members, to serve God.

There is a small group of young people, teenagers

I believe. Some are just visiting with each other while some are busy playing with their smart phones and texting friends. I guess they needed a place to gather, for it doesn't seem as though they are here to come and praise God.

How do you see yourself? Did you come to worship the Lord or be a bench warmer?

How do you think God sees you?

We have angels watching over us at all times in everything we do and say.

MY LOVING GRANDMOTHER

My parents separated when I was a year old. My mother put me into a local orphanage to be adopted. My father found out what she had done and removed me from there and took me to a loving foster home. I remember those loving people and the inside of the house arrangement as if it were yesterday.

I was in the foster home from age one through age six. A strange lady came and took me away and I was to call her Mother. I had no idea what the word "mother" meant. At the same time, I also received a very large grandmother, some cousins and aunts and uncles. The cousins were all near my age, so we could play together.

Now, my grandmother was big – I mean, big! My cousin, who lived next door to her, and I could not reach around her together. She always had good things to eat, her house always smelled of goodies. She couldn't speak very good English, but enough that we could make out what she was saying to us. She had a black book that she read a lot and she took special good care of it. My cousin and I kept asking her what that book was and why did she read it so much. She told us it was a storybook about a very special person. He was her friend and He is also our friend. We couldn't see or hear him, but he was always able to hear and see us all of the time. She said that he loved us very much and that he was our very best friend, too. She told us that he was able to

94

hear everything we say, so we can talk to him, we just couldn't hear him talk back to us. His name was Jesus and he would help us when we are in trouble. We couldn't hide from him – he could still see us.

Even with her broken English, we were able to understand what she was telling us. We believed her and asked no more questions.

When I was bad – and sometimes when I hadn't done anything wrong – my mother would lock me up in the smokehouse. It was dark and smelly in there. She would leave me in there for many hours at a time. Sometimes I would be in there after dark and then I would really get scared. So, I learned to talk to my new invisible friend. My grandma had told me that he could hear me and help me when I got in trouble. Suddenly, I wouldn't be afraid any more. I would sing to myself and sit down in a corner and go to sleep.

Jesus was helping me even when I knew nothing about Him or who He really was. I just knew I wasn't afraid anymore when I talked to Him – I was no longer alone.

I was 16 when I invited Jesus into my life. I was going to church once in a while with a neighbor kid and the preacher kept telling me that I would go to Hell and burn up if I didn't ask Jesus into my heart. I didn't want to burn up, so that was the best way out of that. It was the first time I really felt loved. I was so excited, I wanted to tell everyone I saw.

I have grown and matured over the years and have really gotten to know Jesus and now I serve Him and love Him with all my heart.

I remember my grandmother telling me about my invisible friend and thanked her. I thanked God, too, for giving her to me.

I was 10 years old when my grandmother went home to be with the Lord. I wasn't allowed to tell her goodbye although my cousins did, and we were all around the same age. I could not understand why I had to stay in the car for the funeral and graveside services, but I know one day I will see her again in Heaven and then I can give her the biggest hug ever and tell her "Thank you" for telling me about Jesus.

Grandmothers are very special people. Cherish them.

EPILOGUE

So many times in our prayer time, we are so zeroed in on asking God to do things, we forget the things He has already given to us,

When He doesn't answer us, it isn't that He hasn't heard or has forgotten us, It is because he feels that we are not ready, spiritually, to receive that answer yet.

Everything is already provided for us. It is His will to determine when we are ready and can handle the things we are asking for.

It is God's time, not ours. Many times the answers are much greater for us. He has something greater to give us than what we are asking.

We also forget to thank Him for the things He already has given to us – both the good and the bad... yes, even the bad times. They are the teaching, learning and growing times for us.

We must have patience and wait upon the Lord, listening for His direction.

Keep your eyes and mind on the things of God.
Pray without ceasing.
God is in charge, at all times, over all things!
Praise and Worship 24/7.
God makes a way where there is no way.
Know God and make Him known.
Do you have an attitude or aptitude heart?

OTHER PUBLISHED WORKS
BY JESSIE SCHLASER

Wait, Listen, Record:
Habakkuk 2:1-3

Jessie Schlaser exemplifies Jesus' words in *Matthew* 25, "Then the King will say to those on His right. 'Come, you who are blessed by my Father, take your inheritance, the kingdom prepared for you since the creation of the world. For I was hungry and you gave me something to drink, I was a stranger and you invited me in, I needed clothes and you clothed me, I was sick and you looked after me, I was in prison and you came to visit me. I tell you the truth, whatever you did for the least of these brothers of mine, you did for me."

Caring for the least of these has been Jessie's life. Now she shares that life with you in words of wisdom and encouragement she received from God in some of her darkest hours of personal pain and in testimonies of God's power manifest in her life and through her in the lives of others.and inspired in your own daily life, whatever stage of life you are in and whatever you are going through."

Grandma's Road to Inspiration

Join Jessie Schlaser in her collection of inspirational poetry and stories that she so generously shares with her readers.

Here is a sample from *Grandma's Road to Inspiration* for you to enjoy:

A DOG'S PRAYER

Treat me kindly, my beloved master, for no heart in the world is more grateful for kindness than the loving heart of me. Do not break my spirit with a stick, for though I lick your hand between blows, your patience and understanding will more quickly teach me the things you would have me do.

Speak to me often, for your voice is the world's sweetest music, as you must know by the fierce wagging of my tail when your footstep falls upon my waiting ear.

When it is cold and wet, please take me inside, for I am now a domesticated animal, no longer used to bitter elements. And I ask no greater glory than the privilege of sitting at your feet beside the hearth. Though had you no home, I would rather follow you through ice and snow than rest upon the softest pillow in the warmest home in all the land, for you are my god, and I am your devoted worshiper.

Keep my pan filled with fresh water, for although I should not reproach you were it dry, I cannot tell you when I suffer thirst. Feed me clean food, that I may be well, to romp and play and do your bidding, to walk by your side, and stand ready, willing and able to protect you with my life should your life be in danger.

And, beloved master, should the Great Master see fit to deprive me of my health or sight, do not tum me away from you. Rather, hold my gently in your arms as skilled hands grant me the merciful boon of eternal rest....and I will leave you knowing with the last breath I drew, my fate was ever safest in your hands.

Another example of Jessie's work:

AN ODE TO HARRY TRUMAN
(of Mt. St. Helens fame)

Here's to a big man, just an ordinary man,
he wasn't known to the world,
as such was our late President Truman;
but he was just as noble and human.
He stood tall and strong in his beliefs.
He spoke freely of his thoughts; our freedom of
speech.
He was true to his land to the end; freedom of rights.
He was faithful to his wife; till death do us part.

The mountain rumbled and the mountain roared.
People laughed and peopled scorned
at that senile old man of the ravishing mountain.
He was as true an American
as any man I hope to know.
As he stood for what we all take for granted
and proudly live by every day of our lives.
The freedoms of speech, belief and rights
and the pursuit of happiness.

Harry's spirit will live on
in the generations to come.
And in the hearts and minds of us
that had the privilege to have known him.
I salute you, Harry Truman, Man of the Mountain;
A great American as you were,
Old Man of the Mountain.

By Jessie Schlaser

Jessie's books can be found on-line at Amazon.com and most on-line booksellers.

She maintains eStores for both of her most recent books at:

Grandma's Road to Inspiration
https://www.createspace.com/4479531

and

Fly Like an Eagle
https://www.createspace.com/5967862

Contact the author:

Jessie Schlaser
c/o Groundwaters Publishing, LLC
P.O. Box 50, Lorane, OR 97451

Made in the USA
Columbia, SC
06 June 2020